Full Faith and Credit

Full Faith and Credit

THE LAWYER'S CLAUSE OF THE CONSTITUTION

By ROBERT H. JACKSON
ASSOCIATE JUSTICE OF THE SUPREME
COURT OF THE UNITED STATES

COLUMBIA UNIVERSITY PRESS

NEW YORK · 1945

COPYRIGHT 1945 BY COLUMBIA UNIVERSITY PRESS, NEW YORK
Foreign agent: OXFORD UNIVERSITY PRESS, Humphrey Milford,
Amen House, London, E.C. 4, England, AND B. I. Building,
Nicol Road, Bombay, India

MANUFACTURED IN THE UNITED STATES OF AMERICA

Full Faith and Credit, the Lawyer's Clause of the Constitution, is the fourth annual Benjamin N. Cardozo Lecture, delivered December 7, 1944, before the Association of the Bar of the City of New York, under the auspices of its Committee on Post-Admission Legal Education.

The memory of Benjamin N. Cardozo's life, it is hoped, may be revered and forever shared by the members of this Association and of our profession generally, who may reap from it "something far more precious than pride in his accomplishment and the suggestion of claiming him as our own, namely, that spiritual harvest which comes from the example of an unblemished character," a rare character that radiated goodness, that was inspired by a love for the law, a passion for justice and a sympathy for humanity.
—From the *Report* of the Committee on Post-Admission Legal Education of the Association of the Bar of the City of New York, March 15, 1940.

Other lectures in the series are: *The Influence of Judge Cardozo on the Common Law,* by Irving Lehman, LL.D., Chief Judge, Court of Appeals, State of New York, 1941; *Reason and Fiat in Case Law,* by Lon L. Fuller, J.D., Professor of Law, Harvard Law School, 1942; *The Personality of the Judge,* by Bernard L. Shientag, LL.D., Justice, Supreme Court, State of New York, First Judicial District, 1943.

A namesake lecture [1] in memory of Mr. Justice Cardozo is an undertaking of more than ordinary challenge to a Justice of a succeeding generation. Even choice of a fitting subject has difficulties. One related to the work of the Court on which he and I both have served might seem appropriate. But Judge Cardozo's most significant contributions to the law are not to be found in the reports of the Supreme Court. He was pre-eminently a devotee of the common law, while the Supreme Court has never been distinguished as a source of common law and during his time renounced independence of judgment as to what the common law is or should be in the class of cases that most often invoked it.[2] Its preoccupation with constitutional law and statutory construction caused him some discontent, which was not always concealed. He once said to me, "If you have a chance

---

[1] Reprinted from the *Columbia Law Review*, XLV (January, 1945), 1–34. A report of the address also appeared in *New York Law Journal*, Dec. 18, 1944, p. 1739.

[2] Erie R. Co. v. Tompkins, 304 U. S. 64 (1938). Mr. Justice Cardozo was ill and did not participate in this decision. I have no reason to doubt that he was sympathetic with the desire to overcome the evils of the *Swift v. Tyson* doctrine. The opinion, however, seems to assume that the process of judging state law by a federal court can be so mechanical that without the use of judgment of its own it can pick out and apply state precedents which determine the law of the state. If I read Judge Cardozo aright, he had no thought that the process of finding decisional law could be so simplified. See, for example, CARDOZO, THE NATURE OF THE JUDICIAL PROCESS (1921) 64 *et seq.*

[2]

to go on the New York Court of Appeals, by all means do so. It is a great common law court, its problems are lawyers' problems. But the Supreme Court is occupied chiefly with statutory construction—which no man can make interesting—and with politics." Politics, I hasten to say, was used in the sense of policy, not of partisanship, and had no derogatory implications.

To decide cases merely by application of statutory law, he long before had written, involves "a process of search, comparison, and little more," and "If that were all there was to our calling, there would be little of intellectual interest about it." Statutory interpretation has indeed its problems, but he felt that "they lack at times some of that element of mystery which accompanies creative energy. We reach the land of mystery when constitution and statute are silent, and the judge must look to the common law for the rule that fits the case." [3] On the other hand constitutional questions often leave the judge without the steadying guidance of the common law, and much turns "upon the social or juridical philosophies of the judges who constitute the court at one time or another." [4]

So the Supreme Court, engrossed as it is with questions of public law, did not draw upon his special store of intellectual treasures so constantly or so gratefully as did the New York Court of Appeals.

[3] CARDOZO, THE NATURE OF THE JUDICIAL PROCESS (1921) 18–21.
[4] Lecture delivered before New York State Bar Association, January 22, 1932. 55 Reports N. Y. State Bar Ass'n (1932) 281.

[3]

His views of the nature of the judicial process and of its functions in the growth of the law were fully matured before he went upon the Supreme Court.[5] But its unique role and method must have provoked meditations in his prolific mind that would have enriched our literature if he had taken occasion to divulge them to the profession.

However, the Supreme Court deals with one clause of the Constitution which seems to me peculiarly a lawyer's clause, and its problems must have appealed to the lawyerly intuitions of Judge Cardozo. The first paragraph of what often is called the Federal Article reads, "Full Faith and Credit shall be given in each State to the public Acts, Records and judicial Proceedings of every other State. And the Congress may by general Laws prescribe the Manner in which such Acts, Records and Proceedings shall be proved, and the Effect thereof." This clause involves a constitutional aspect of what Judge Cardozo called "one of the most baffling subjects of legal science, the so-called *Conflict of Law*."[6] Its interpretation is less involved than that of most constitutional provisions with social and political considera-

---

[5] His THE NATURE OF THE JUDICIAL PROCESS was published in 1921; THE GROWTH OF THE LAW, 1924; PARADOXES OF LEGAL SCIENCE, 1928; LAW AND LITERATURE AND OTHER ESSAYS, 1931; and his lecture *The Judicial Process up to Now* was delivered to the New York State Bar Association, January 22, 1932. He was commissioned a Justice of the Supreme Court, March 2, 1932. His lecture to the State Bar Association stands somewhat as his testament to the legal profession. See note 4, *supra*.
[6] CARDOZO, THE PARADOXES OF LEGAL SCIENCE (1928) 67.

[4]

tions. It is concerned with the techniques of the law. It serves to co-ordinate the administration of justice among the several independent legal systems which exist in our federation.

This clause is relatively neglected in legal literature. It did not have the advantage of early and luminous exposition by Marshall. No scholar has thought it worthy of a book. Text writers have usually noticed it only as a subsidiary consideration in the law of conflicts or as a phase of constitutional law too obvious to require much exploration. Changing conditions of a century and a half have brought forth no new legislative implementation. The practicing lawyer often neglects to raise questions under it, and judges not infrequently decide cases to which it would apply without mention of it.[7]

For these reasons I hope to stimulate, rather than to satisfy, inquiry upon a subject which has impressed me as being both important and obscure to the profession.

THE WRITTEN LAW OF FULL FAITH AND CREDIT

The Constitutional Convention of 1787 found the basic faith and credit provision as to judgments al-

---

[7] Loucks v. Standard Oil Co., 224 N. Y. 99, 120 N. E. 198 (1918), is an example. It was an action to recover damages for death by negligence. The accident occurred in Massachusetts. Suit was in New York, and it was claimed the Massachusetts statute as to damages applied. It allowed punitive damages. The issue was tendered only as a matter of state conflict of laws. Cardozo, J., decided the case without mention of the full faith and credit clause. See also

[5]

ready in the Articles of Confederation.[8] If we turn back to the Continental Congress which put it in the Articles of Confederation, the record leaves its conception obscure, but indicates that its period of gestation was something under five days. Neither the Franklin draft [9] nor the Dickinson draft [10] of the proposed Articles contained anything like it. On November 10, 1777, Congress appointed a committee to consider "sundry propositions" that had been laid before it.[11] The following day the committee proposed new articles, one of which was a full faith and credit clause. A provision that an action of debt may lie in the court of any state to recover on the judgment of another was rejected.[12] The basic pro-

---

Colorado v. Harbeck, 232 N. Y. 71, 133 N. E. 357 (1921); Moore v. Mitchell, 28 F.(2d) 997 (S. D. N. Y. 1928), 30 F.(2d) 600 (C. C. A. 2d, 1929); Fox v. Postal Telegraph-Cable Co., 138 Wis. 648, 120 N. W. 399 (1909).

[8] "Full faith and credit shall be given in each of these States to the records, acts and judicial proceedings of the courts and magistrates of every other State." ARTICLES OF CONFEDERATION, ART. IV.

[9] AMERICAN HISTORY LEAFLETS, No. 20 (July 21, 1775) 3.

[10] *Id.* at 8 (July 12, 1776).

[11] The committee consisted of Richard Law, Richard Henry Lee, and James Duane. 9 JOURNALS OF THE CONTINENTAL CONGRESS (1907) 885.

[12] The proposed article read: "That full Faith and Credit shall be given in each of these States to the Records, Acts, and Judicial Proceedings of the Courts and Magistrates of every other State, and that an Action of Debt may lie in the Court of Law in any State for the Recovery of a Debt due on Judgment of any Court in any other State; provided the Judgment Creditor gives sufficient Bond with Sureties before Said Court before whom Action is brought to respond in Damages to the Adverse Party in Case the original Judgment Should be afterwards reversed and Set aside." A footnote in the published *Journals* records that the report was in the handwriting of Richard Law and that the part concerning an

[6]

vision was adopted and included in the final draft of the Articles, enacted four days later.[13]

My research is necessarily inadequate and does not disclose the real origin of the proposal, and I am doubtful if now it is discoverable.[14] Who was its real author? Did he copy or adapt some earlier model? Was the proposal to create causes of action on judgments rejected because the Congress did not approve that procedure, or was it considered so well established as to need no mention? [15] All these interesting questions I leave unanswered.

The Constitutional Convention of 1787 extended the confederation provision to include nonjudicial "public" acts and records, which the Articles had not mentioned, and it empowered Congress by general laws to "prescribe the manner in which such acts, records and proceedings shall be proved, and the effect thereof." Debate on this subject as recorded was brief and cryptic and participated in by but a few

---

action of debt was "struck out in Congress." *Id.* at 887 and n. 5. The following day the faith and credit portion was adopted, but an attempt to add the action of debt provision failed, all members of the committee voting against it. *Id.* at 895–96.

[13] *Id.* at 907.

[14] See BURNETT, THE CONTINENTAL CONGRESS (1941); JENSEN, THE ARTICLES OF CONFEDERATION (1940). See also Radin, *The Authenticated Full Faith and Credit Clause: Its History* (1944) 39 ILL. L. REV. 1.

[15] The law upon this subject as understood at the time is reviewed by Mr. Justice Gray in Hilton v. Guyot, 159 U. S. 113, 180 (1895). It shows both that judgments often were given *prima facie* effect only and that some colonies had taken measures to prevent their impeachment. It also shows early difference of opinion among authorities as to the meaning of the full faith and credit provision.

[7]

delegates,[16] but statements reveal something of the thought of those who led the Convention's action on this clause. The significance of what they said will be more apparent as we go along. "Mr. Wilson & Docr. Johnson supposed the meaning to be that Judgments in one State should be the ground of actions in other States, & that acts of the Legislatures should be included, for the sake of Acts of insolvency &c." [17]

The proposal then under consideration conferred no power on Congress, and Mr. Madison supported committing it for reconsideration. "He wished the Legislature might be authorized to provide for the *execution* of Judgments in other States, under such regulations as might be expedient— He thought that this might be safely done and was justified by the nature of the Union." [18] Gouverneur Morris moved also to commit a proposition that "the Legislature shall by general laws, determine the proof and effect of such acts, records, and proceedings." [19] His motion was adopted, and when next reported the clause included such a provision. On further debate Mr. Wilson remarked that "if the Legislature were not allowed to *declare the effect* the provision would amount to nothing more than what now takes place

---

[16] The proceedings are set forth in 2 FARRAND, THE RECORDS OF THE FEDERAL CONVENTION (1911) 188, 447–48, 484–86, 488–89, reviewed and commented upon in COOK, THE LOGICAL AND LEGAL BASES OF THE CONFLICT OF LAWS (1942) 90; Costigan, *The History of the Adoption of Section 1 of Article IV* (1904) 4 COLUMBIA LAW REV. 470.
[17] 2 FARRAND, *op. cit. supra* note 16 at 447.
[18] *Id.* at 448.   [19] *Ibid.*

[8]

among all Independent Nations." [20] The opposition came from Mr. Randolph who expressed fear "that its definition of the powers of the Government was so loose as to give it opportunities of usurping all the State powers." [21] His fears, however, did not prevail, and the whole clause was carried substantially in its present form.

Contemporary expositions of the Constitution, such as *The Federalist* [22] and the debates of the ratifying conventions, throw little more light than this on just what the forefathers had in mind to accomplish by the clause.

The First Congress, in 1790, prescribed a manner of authenticating legislative acts and of proving judicial proceedings. It declared that "records and judicial proceedings authenticated as aforesaid, shall have such faith and credit given to them in every court within the United States, as they have by law or usage in the courts of the state from whence the said records are or shall be taken." [23] In 1804 Congress

---

[20] 2 FARRAND, *op. cit. supra* note 16 at 488. [21] *Id.* at 489.

[22] *The Federalist* was content with mere assertion that this clause is "an evident and valuable improvement on the clause relating to this subject in the articles of Confederation" and that the power "may be rendered a very convenient instrument of justice, and be particularly beneficial on the borders of contiguous States." But Madison includes this little notice of the clause in his discussion of powers "which provide for the harmony and proper intercourse among the States." THE FEDERALIST, No. 42.

[23] Act of May 26, 1790, 1 STAT. 122. The *Annals of Congress* record only that on April 28, 1790, Mr. John Page of Virginia, "from the committee appointed for the purpose," presented the bill to provide for authentication, that it was twice read and committed, read the

[9]

added a method of exemplification of nonjudicial records and prescribed their effect in similar terms.[24] In substance these two Acts still remain the statutory law.[25] They constitute the entire contribution of Congress to the evolution of our law of faith and credit. What became of Madison's desire that Congress legislate for *execution* of state judgments throughout the Union? Why did Congress make no attempt to say when or how statutes or decisional law are to be given effect in states other than the one of origin? With such meager constitutional and statutory materials the courts were left to work out the concrete application of the clause.

Like most written law, these provisions of Constitution and statute were "built upon a substratum of common law, modifying, in details only, the com-

---

third time and passed on May 3, and that it was read the third time in the Senate and passed on May 5. 1 ANNALS OF CONG. 969; 2 *id.* at 1548, 1550.

[24] Act of March 27, 1804, 2 STAT. 298. Available legislative history is not more enlightening as to this Act. It is recorded that on motion of Mr. Joseph H. Nicholson of Maryland it was resolved by the House that a committee be appointed to inquire and report, by bill or otherwise, whether it was necessary to add to the Act any provisions for authentication of judicial records. Nov. 1, 1803, ANNALS OF CONG., 8th Cong., 1st Sess., 554. A bill was reported the following day, was debated and, "after considerable discussion, developing much diversity of opinion," was recommitted on November 25. *Id.* at 555, 626. February 7, 1804, a new bill was reported which was passed without amendment on March 23 and was passed by the Senate March 27. *Id.* at 979, 1226, 1227, 299, 304, 306. Since no debate is recorded, the causes of disagreement cannot be known, but the bill in its original and final forms varied only in details of expression.

[25] 28 U. S. C. §§ 687, 688 (1940).

[10]

mon law foundation." [26] Perhaps the meaning of the clause could better be appraised if we could better recapture or reconstruct the relevant common-law doctrines of "private international law" which presumably entered into the thinking of the forefathers. But the literature on this subject at the close of the eighteenth century was unorganized and unsystematic. As late as 1834, in the preface to his pioneer book on Conflict of Laws, Joseph Story complained about the loose and scattered condition of the materials and about the difficulty of treating his subject. He said, "There exists no treatise upon it in the English language; and not the slightest effort has been made, except by Mr. Chancellor Kent, to arrange in any general order even the more familiar maxims of the common law in regard to it." I am not confident that the efforts of Justices to restate the early law as it appeared to the forefathers is either complete or accurate.[27] Often Judges are not thorough or objective historians. I find no satisfactory evidence that the members of the Constitutional Convention or the early Congresses had more than a hazy knowledge of the problems they sought to settle or of those which they created by the faith and credit clause.[28] Certainly they did not anticipate the refinements and distinctions that have been developed by later experience and now find place in

[26] CARDOZO, THE GROWTH OF THE LAW (1924) 136.
[27] *Cf.* M'Elmoyle v. Cohen, 13 Pet. 312 (U. S. 1839); Hilton v. Guyot, 159 U. S. 113, 180 (1895).
[28] Kent's *Commentaries* did not appear until 1826.

[11]

that peculiarly American body of scholarship and controversy known as "Conflict of Laws." However, to define the exact extent of the federal obligation upon the states to recognize public acts, records, and judicial proceedings of sister states which the founders substituted for whatever voluntary recognition was then practiced has been one of the recurring problems of the Supreme Court.

JUDICIAL DEVELOPMENT OF THE CLAUSE AS TO JUDGMENTS

Not until 1813 was the Supreme Court called upon to consider the faith and credit clause and statutes. Then, Francis Scott Key, in his almost forgotten role of advocate, contended that merely to receive in evidence a judgment from another state to be weighed with other evidence gave to it all the faith and credit required. The Court said, however, through Mr. Justice Story, that such an interpretation would render the clause "utterly unimportant and illusory" and held that a judgment conclusive in the state where rendered must be received as conclusive elsewhere.[29] But Mr. Justice Story gave no exposition of the philosophy of the clause. A few years later Chief Justice Marshall, in a single paragraph, applied it to a case, foregoing the opportunity to expound its doctrine in his imperishable

[29] Mills v. Duryee, 7 Cranch 481 (U. S. 1813). Key appears to have cited no authority for his argument, and his less noted adversary, Jones, cited only the interesting decision of Justice Wilson at circuit in Armstrong v. Carson, 2 Dall. 302 (U. S. 1794).

[12]

phrase.[30] Unfortunately, another twenty years were to pass before the Court found occasion to make extended commentary on the clause. Meanwhile the slavery question had begun to distort men's views of government and of law. Talk of "state sovereignty" became involved in the issue. The Taney Court wrote in a spirit hard to reconcile with the spirit of the short but uncompromising opinion written for the Marshall Court by Mr. Justice Story.[31] Although he was still a member of the Court, he did not dissent. Perhaps he disagreed, as he frequently did, with his associates who were products of the Jacksonian era, but did not carry the difference beyond the conference room. Perhaps he was placated by being several times cited as an authority.

I shall not review subsequent cases as to judgments, which constitute the bulk of faith and credit litigation, further than roughly to indicate where we stand today. Despite the sweeping language used in both clause and statute, the course of later interpretation may be summed up in language of Chief Justice Stone that "the full faith and credit clause is not an inexorable and unqualified command." [32] Qualifications which time has introduced as to judgments *in personam* we may conveniently group under four principal heads:

1. The most important and perhaps the least

[30] Hampton v. M'Connel, 3 Wheat. 234 (U. S. 1818).
[31] M'Elmoyle v. Cohen, 13 Pet. 312 (U. S. 1839).
[32] Pink v. A. A. A. Highway Express, Inc., 314 U. S. 201, 210 (1941).

[13]

questionable is that a forum may go back of a foreign judgment to inquire whether the rendering court had jurisdiction. The question whether evidence may be received to contradict the record as to jurisdictional facts did not reach the Supreme Court, strangely enough, until 1873. The Court held that jurisdiction always is open to inquiry [33] and later said "it must be taken to be established that a court cannot conclude all persons interested by its mere assertion of its own power, even where its power depends upon a fact and it finds the fact." [34] The qualification means little more than that before receiving a judgment with conclusive effect a court

---

[33] Thompson v. Whitman, 18 Wall. 457, 468 (U. S. 1873); Bell v. Bell, 181 U. S. 175 (1901); National Exchange Bank v. Wiley, 195 U. S. 257, 270 (1904). Jurisdiction is tacitly asserted, even if not expressly, by the fact of rendering judgment. Chicago Life Ins. Co. v. Cherry, 244 U. S. 25, 29 (1917). While jurisdiction will always be presumed until the contrary appears, the defendant is entitled to the advantage of any defects which appear in the record, notwithstanding recitals in the judgment to the contrary. Settlemier v. Sullivan, 97 U. S. 444 (1878). If the rendering state treats a judgment as *res judicata* of jurisdiction provided the question has been litigated, the enforcing state is at liberty to give recognition to that effect without denying due process. Chicago Life Ins. Co. v. Cherry, *supra*. Whether the enforcing state is required to do so was reserved. It is the rule for federal courts that such a judgment is *res judicata*. Baldwin v. Iowa State Traveling Men's Ass'n., 283 U. S. 522 (1931); American Surety Co. v. Baldwin, 287 U. S. 156 (1932); Treinies v. Sunshine Mining Co., 308 U. S. 66 (1939); see Medina, *Conclusiveness of Rulings on Jurisdiction* (1931) 31 COLUMBIA LAW REV. 238; Farrier, *Full Faith and Credit of Adjudication of Jurisdictional Facts* (1935) 2 U. OF CHI. L. REV. 552; Boskey and Braucher, *Jurisdiction and Collateral Attack: October Term, 1939* (1940) 40 COLUMBIA LAW REV. 1006.

[34] Chicago Life Ins. Co. v. Cherry, 244 U. S. 25, 29 (1917).

[14]

may make sure whether it is the genuine judgment it purports to be. Of course, if a tribunal has not jurisdiction to render a judgment valid by the tests of due process, it is without validity at home and is entitled to no credit abroad.[35] To give conclusive effect to such a judgment would in itself be a denial of due process. It is under this head that most of the litigations concerning faith and credit occur.[36]

[35] Pennoyer v. Neff, 95 U. S. 714 (1877); Old Wayne Mutual Life Ass'n. v. McDonough, 204 U. S. 8 (1907); Wetmore v. Karrick, 205 U. S. 141 (1907); Riverside Mills v. Menefee, 237 U. S. 189 (1915).

[36] Jurisdictional questions that have arisen are many, but a few examples will illustrate the principles of decision. A judgment may be denied credit upon showing lack of personal service where there is no other ground for jurisdiction of the person. Pennoyer v. Neff, 95 U. S. 714 (1877); Wetmore v. Karrick, 205 U. S. 141 (1907). But it is not clear whether faith and credit could be denied on evidence of no personal service where a sheriff's return showed service and local law provided that it might not be impeached. A judgment rendered on such a return is held not to be void for denial of due process, at least in a foreclosure proceeding against land lying within the state. Miedreich v. Lauenstein, 232 U. S. 236 (1914). See Farrier, *Full Faith and Credit of Adjudications of Jurisdictional Facts* (1935) 2 U. OF CHI. L. REV. 552, 560; Medina, *Conclusiveness of Rulings on Jurisdiction* (1931) 31 COLUMBIA LAW REV. 238, 241. Where jurisdiction is founded solely on consent, such as an authorization to confess judgment sometimes found in promissory notes or bonds, the judgment will not be given faith and credit if it is shown that the terms of the authorization were not strictly followed. Grover & Baker Sewing Machine Co. v. Radcliffe, 137 U. S. 287 (1890); National Exchange Bank v. Wiley, 195 U. S. 257 (1904); see Note, *Full Faith and Credit for Judgments Confessed by Attorney* (1931) 44 HARV. L. REV. 1275. A voluntary general appearance of course confers jurisdiction of the person, but in some states that consequence also is attributed to a special appearance for the limited purpose of contesting jurisdiction. This paradoxical result is held not to deny due process of law, and hence it probably would not be grounds for a denial of faith and credit. York v. Texas, 137 U. S. 15 (1890); Kauffman v. Wootters, 138 U. S.

2. The Court has distinguished between a plea to the merits of a judgment, as to which it is held invincible, and a plea to the remedy, as to which it is held subject to the law of the forum. Distinguishing between denial of a right and denial of a remedy is a rather academic enterprise and not a thoroughly satisfying one. But on that basis it is held that a suit upon a judgment is subject to the statute of limitations of the forum state, rather than to that of the rendering state.[37]

3. It has been held that a state is not required to provide a remedy on a judgment rendered in a sister state when both parties are foreign corporations.[38] This exception, under the doctrine of *forum non*

---

285 (1891); Western Life Indemnity Co. v. Rupp, 235 U. S. 261 (1914). On consequences of special appearance, see Farrier, *supra* at 552, 567. Domicile of an individual or doing business within a state by a corporation often are relied upon to empower courts of the state to obtain personal jurisdiction without personal service of process therein. One may sometimes discredit a judgment rendered on substituted service by showing that at the time he was not domiciled in the jurisdiction. Cooper v. Newell, 173 U. S. 555, 569 (1899). And a corporation may contest the finding that it was present in the state by engaging in business therein. For a collection of cases, see Farmers' & Merchants' Bank v. Federal Reserve Bank, 286 Fed. 566 (E. D. Ky. 1922); 3 FREEMAN ON JUDGMENTS (5th ed. 1925) § 1414. Of course jurisdiction may be grounded *in rem*, in which case jurisdiction over the *res* is subject to inquiry. Thompson v. Whitman, 18 Wall. 457 (U. S. 1873).

[37] M'Elmoyle v. Cohen, 13 Pet. 312 (U. S. 1839); see Campbell v. Holt, 115 U. S. 620 (1885); Davis v. Mills, 194 U. S. 451 (1904); Danzer & Co. v. Gulf & Ship Island R. Co., 268 U. S. 633 (1925); Midstate Horticultural Co. v. Pennsylvania R. Co., 320 U. S. 356 (1943).

[38] Anglo-American Provision Co. v. Davis Provision Co., 191 U. S. 373 (1903).

[16]

conveniens, has been, however, closely limited by later cases.³⁹

4. The faith and credit clause has been held to permit the forum to examine the cause of action merged in the judgment and, if it was based on a penalty, to refuse enforcement.⁴⁰ This, too, has been limited strictly to penalties,⁴¹ and the Court refused to extend the doctrine to a judgment for taxes in an opinion which casts some shadow on the whole penalty exception.⁴²

When Congress failed to provide for universal execution of judgments, as Madison had hoped, it left the practice of suing upon judgment in effect. This was certain to make them vulnerable to procedural peculiarities, and to some extent to local policies, of the forum. The last three exceptions are examples of local policy prevailing over the command that faith and credit be accorded to judicial proceedings of a sister state. Whether there may be other local policies that might prevail, at least as to judgments other than conventional ones for a sum of money, we need not stop to inquire.⁴³

---

³⁹ It is clear that jurisdiction may not be denied merely because the forum state does not recognize the kind of cause of action on which the judgment is based. Fauntleroy v. Lum, 210 U. S. 230 (1908); Kenney v. Supreme Lodge, 252 U. S. 411 (1920); Roche v. McDonald, 275 U. S. 449 (1928); Broderick v. Rosner, 294 U. S. 629 (1935).

⁴⁰ Wisconsin v. Pelican Ins. Co., 127 U. S. 265, 291 (1888).

⁴¹ Huntington v. Attrill, 146 U. S. 657 (1892).

⁴² Milwaukee County v. M. E. White Co., 296 U. S. 268 (1935).

⁴³ See Note, *Extraterritorial Recognition of Injunctions against Suit* (1930) 39 YALE L. J. 719, and discussion in Miles v. Illinois Cent. R. Co., 315 U. S. 698 (1942), and B. & O. R. Co. v. Kepner, 314 U. S.

[17]

On this basis we may generalize as to how near we have approached Madison's suggestion that judgments of a state court be executed in every other state. A money judgment in the usual civil action, if it survives inquiry into jurisdiction of the rendering tribunal, is unimpeachable in a sister state, either as a basis for a judgment of its courts or as a shield against further litigation of the same issues by the same parties. Exceptions there are, but they are few and affect only a small number of judgments, and no tendency to enlarge them appears.

---

44 (1941). Injunctions against prosecuting divorce actions elsewhere, *e.g.*, Holmes v. Holmes, 46 N. Y. S.(2d) 628 (Sup. Ct. 1944), may raise interesting problems of faith and credit. See also Sistare v. Sistare, 218 U. S. 1 (1910), and Barber v. Barber, No. 51, Oct. Term, 1944, decided Dec. 4, 1944 (whether finality requisite for faith and credit); Fall v. Eastin, 215 U. S. 1 (1909) (nonrecognition of foreign decree affecting land within the forum state). The growth of administrative tribunals has given rise to an interesting question as to whether their awards, assessments, and decisions are to be treated as judicial proceedings or as public acts or records. Awards under compensation acts have been treated as judgments. Magnolia Petroleum Co. v. Hunt, 320 U. S. 430 (1943). But it is possible that administrative actions less adjudicatory in nature would be treated differently. See Broderick v. Rosner, 294 U. S. 629, 647 (1935). Some concern resulted from the twice-repeated statement that "it has often been recognized by this Court that there are some limitations upon the extent to which a state may be required by the full faith and credit clause to enforce *even the judgment* of another state in contravention of its own statutes or policy [italics supplied]." Alaska Packers Ass'n. v. Industrial Accident Comm'n, 294 U. S. 532, 546 (1935); Pacific Employers Ins. Co. v. Industrial Accident Comm'n, 306 U. S. 493, 502 (1939). But the effect of this language, at least as to money judgments rendered in civil suits, has been largely dissipated recently. See Williams v. North Carolina, 317 U. S. 287, 294-95 (1942); Magnolia Petroleum Co. v. Hunt, 320 U. S. 430, 438 (1943).

[18]

DECISIONAL LAW AS TO FAITH AND CREDIT FOR STATUTORY AND COMMON LAW

Congress has provided no guidance as to when extraterritorial recognition shall be accorded either to a state's statutes or to its common law. Since the Constitutional provision must now be regarded as self-executing,[44] however, the courts have been obliged to solve issues under it as best they could. So long as the private law of the states was pretty generally common law there was fair uniformity, and whose law applied did not often matter. But as many states began to abrogate the common law with statutory enactments, the choice of law grew in importance, and controversies over it have multiplied.

Questions as to faith and credit for foreign law seem inherently more difficult than questions as to recognition of judgments. There is comparatively little trouble in learning to whom and to what a judgment applies, for that is what the very process of adjudication settles. But the effect to be given to the law of a sister state generally turns on whether the state itself has the right to reach and govern a particular transaction, or property, or person, because of some relationship which confers what roughly may be

[44] Whether it is self-executing has been questioned in state courts. See Langmaid, *The Full Faith and Credit Required for Public Acts* (1929) 24 ILL. L. REV. 383, 388. But see M'Elmoyle v. Cohen, 13 Pet. 312, 325 (U. S. 1839); 2 STORY ON THE CONSTITUTION (5th ed. 1891) 193. In fact, no requirement of faith and credit for statutes exists unless the clause is self-executing. See Bradford Electric Light Co. v. Clapper, 286 U. S. 145 (1932).

[19]

described as "legislative jurisdiction." A state's claim to govern generally is based on some "jurisdictional fact," such as presence of a party within the state, a transaction or event therein to which its law attaches consequences, domicile or citizenship of one or both parties, or place of forum. Conflicting claims often arise because one state has one such jurisdictional relationship, as, let us say, the place of transaction, while a different state is the place of domicile or of forum. Or sometimes the conflicting claims as to governing law are based upon the same ground, as, for example, domicile, with conflicting findings as to which is the state of domicile, or transactions run through several states and each has some claim to govern their legal consequences.

Plainly, quite different inquiries must be made and different principles applied to this class of questions than to issues as to the recognition of judgments. Such questions lead into consideration of the powers of independent and "sovereign" states and the limitations which result from their union in the Federal Compact. These questions are of extraordinary complexity and delicacy.

The Constitution by use of the term "public acts" clearly includes statutes.[45] But it makes no mention of decisional law. However, an underlying point of *Erie v. Tompkins* was that "whether the law of the

---

[45] Bradford Electric Light Co. v. Clapper, 286 U. S. 145, 155 (1932); John Hancock Mutual Life Ins. Co. v. Yates, 299 U. S. 178, 183 (1936).

[20]

State shall be declared by its Legislature in a statute or by its highest court in a decision is not a matter of federal concern." [46] It is not far-fetched to argue that full faith and credit for judicial proceedings requires recognition of their effect as decisional law, if they have that effect in the state where rendered, as well as of their *res judicata* effect. In any event, while the point seems not to have been discussed, the Court has so acted and talked that we may deal with this part of our subject on the assumption that what is entitled in proper cases to credit is the law of a state by whatever source declared.[47]

As to the circumstances under which choice of law may present a federal question, there is old controversy [48] and new confusion. Even before *Erie v. Tompkins* the Court, in a case wherein it was contended that error in a common-law rule of conflicts deprived the litigant of due process of law, had said that a "mistaken application of doctrines of the conflict of laws . . . is a matter with which this court is not concerned," since it is purely a question of local common law.[49] And since *Erie v. Tompkins* the

[46] 304 U. S. 64, 78 (1938).
[47] Royal Arcanum v. Green, 237 U. S. 531 (1915); Modern Woodmen v. Mixer, 267 U. S. 544 (1925); Magnolia Petroleum Co. v. Hunt, 320 U. S. 430, 445 (1943).
[48] See Dodd, *The Power of the Supreme Court to Review State Decisions in the Field of Conflict of Laws* (1926) 39 HARV. L. REV. 533; Langmaid, *The Full Faith and Credit Required for Public Acts* (1929) 24 ILL. L. REV. 383; Ross, *Has the Conflict of Laws Become a Branch of Constitutional Law?* (1931) 15 MINN. L. REV. 161.
[49] Kryger v. Wilson, 242 U. S. 171, 176 (1916).

[21]

Court has held that Federal courts are bound to apply the state decisional law of conflicts in two cases brought into federal court solely because of diversity in the citizenship of parties. In one of the opinions Mr. Justice Reed stated that a state court's choice of law is "Subject only to review by this Court on any federal question that may arise," [50] but rejected the faith and credit argument made in the case with very curt consideration, and in the companion case said that "Where this Court has required the state of the forum to apply the foreign law under the full faith and credit clause or under the Fourteenth Amendment, it has recognized that a state is not required to enforce a law obnoxious to its public policy." [51] This was in 1941. In 1939, for a unanimous Court, Mr. Justice Stone said, "This Court must determine for itself how far the full faith and credit clause compels the qualification or denial of rights asserted under the laws of one state, that of the forum, by the statute of another state." [52] I cannot say with any assurance where the line is drawn today between what the Supreme Court will decide as constitutional law and what it will leave to the states as common law.

Overlapping and conflicting state laws present a problem for which the Court over the years has been

[50] Klaxon Co. v. Stentor Electric Mfg. Co., 313 U. S. 487, 496-97 (1941).
[51] Griffin v. McCoach, 313 U. S. 498, 507 (1941).
[52] Pacific Employers Ins. Co. v. Industrial Accident Comm'n, 306 U. S. 493, 502 (1939).

[22]

groping for solutions and in dealing with which it has not consistently adhered to any fixed principle. A brief survey of the way in which these problems have presented themselves may be worth while.

In the 1880's states began to depart from common-law doctrine and to adopt statutes allowing and regulating recovery for death by negligence. When suit was brought in a state which did not permit such a recovery under its own law, the question arose whether the forum must permit recovery by following the law of the state where the accident occurred. The Supreme Court held that it must; but it is to be noted that neither counsel nor the Court relied on the full faith and credit clause, but on the common-law principles of conflict.[53] Those were the days when the Court saw no wrong in deciding common-law questions for itself, and it is hard to say what would have been the outcome had *Erie v. Tompkins* been the rule at the time. Some states attempted to restrict suit under their death statutes to their own courts. This soon presented the question whether such a restriction required forums of other states to relinquish cases brought therein on such foreign statutes. This was presented and decided as a federal question. It was held that forum states need not observe that limitation,[54] a result which troubled

[53] Dennick v. Railroad Co., 103 U. S. 11 (1880); Stewart v. B. & O. R. Co., 168 U. S. 445 (1897); Northern Pacific R. Co. v. Babcock, 154 U. S. 190 (1894).
[54] Atcheson, T. & S. F. Ry. Co. v. Sowers, 213 U. S. 55 (1909); Tennessee Coal, Iron & R. Co. v. George, 233 U. S. 354 (1914).

[23]

Mr. Justice Holmes, who dissented, but not on constitutional grounds.

In two other classes of cases—those against corporations arising out of relations to stockholders and those against insurance companies growing out of relations to policyholders—the Court has sometimes interfered with state choice of law, requiring in some that the controversies be adjudged according to the statutes and decisions of the chartering state, in others merely refusing to allow adjudication by the law of the forum.[55]

Questions of faith and credit in matrimonial relations have usually come up only as to the effect of judgments.[56] But not infrequently these cast in terms of a jurisdictional issue what might have been an underlying question of choice of law if raised at an earlier state of the litigation. If one of the parties to a marriage leaves the state of matrimonial domicile to seek a divorce elsewhere, a defendant might well answer—if obliged to answer at all—that such

[55] Converse v. Hamilton, 224 U. S. 243 (1912); Royal Arcanum v. Green, 237 U. S. 531 (1915); Modern Woodmen v. Mixer, 267 U. S. 544 (1924); Broderick v. Rosner, 294 U. S. 629 (1935); Chandler v. Peketz, 297 U. S. 609 (1936).

New York Life Ins. Co. v. Head, 234 U. S. 149 (1914); New York Life Ins. Co. v. Dodge, 246 U. S. 357 (1918); Aetna Life Ins. Co. v. Dunken, 266 U. S. 389 (1924); Home Ins. Co. v. Dick, 281 U. S. 397 (1930); Hartford Accident & Indemnity Co. v. Delta & Pine Land Co., 292 U. S. 143 (1934).

[56] Cf. Bell v. Bell, 181 U. S. 175 (1901); Haddock v. Haddock, 201 U. S. 562 (1906); Sistare v. Sistare, 218 U. S. 1 (90); Yarborough v. Yarborough, 290 U. S. 202 (1933); Williams v. North Carolina, 317 U. S. 287 (1942); Esenwein v. Pennsylvania, No. 20, Oct. Term 1944.

[24]

forum must give full faith and credit to the statutes of the state of actual domicile.[57] The whole issue of faith and credit as applied to the law of domestic relations is difficult, and the books of the Court will not be closed on it for a long time, if ever.

Two choice-of-law rulings have been made by the Supreme Court, each reversing the application of a state liability statute to nondelivery of telegrams undertaken to be delivered in places under federal jurisdiction.[58] The decisions do not make it clear whether they go on the ground of an erroneous conflict of laws decision or on conflict with the federal commerce power. If the faith and credit clause is to be applied to choice of law in contracts, troublesome and multitudinous cases will be subject to federal review. It is hard, however, to see why contract cases should be excluded from the benefits of a provision intended to adapt our legal systems to the needs of a national commerce.[59]

---

[57] See COOK, THE LOGICAL AND LEGAL BASES OF THE CONFLICT OF LAWS (1942) 463–64.

[58] Western Union Tel. Co. v. Chiles, 214 U. S. 274 (1909); Western Union Tel. Co. v. Brown, 234 U. S. 542 (1914).

[59] Compare the much-discussed decision in Fox v. Postal Telegraph-Cable Co., 138 Wis. 648, 120 N.W. 399 (1909). In New York City a New York corporation accepted a telegram for transmission to Chicago under the terms of its undertaking. The message was sent unrepeated and subject to the stipulation that for delay in delivery the company should be liable only to refund the price of the message. Delivery was delayed. The sender sued the company for substantial damages in Wisconsin court. It does not appear that either the sender or the addressee was a citizen or domiciliary of Wisconsin, that the message concerned any property located or affairs pending in Wisconsin, or that the message at any point of

[25]

Another field where conflicting state laws sometimes present questions of faith and credit is taxation. Of course, overlapping or double taxation does not necessarily involve faith and credit issues; but in some cases that might involve such issues, counsel fail to raise that question, relying sometimes on other grounds, such as denial of due process. How far a state may call upon other states to aid it in extraterritorial pursuit of revenues, I do not know. New York State courts and the federal courts sitting therein have refused to reduce the tax law of other states to judgment,[60] and the reasons have been set forth in able opinions by Judges Pound, Learned Hand, and Knox. But the Supreme Court has since held that, if the state reduces its claim to judgment,

---

its transmission passed through Wisconsin. The stipulation for limited liability was valid under the law both of New York, where the contract was made, and of Illinois, where the message was delivered. The Wisconsin court held the limitation odious to the public policy of Wisconsin and unenforceable in its courts. It did not, however, dismiss the action, but proceeded under its own law to adjudge the imported controversy and rendered judgment for substantial damages. What it did was to apply a law foreign to the place of transaction to create a new contract and to adjudge a liability that was not imposed by the law of any place where any of the transactions took place. But the case seems to have been submitted by counsel without raising and to have been decided by the court without considering the implications of the Constitutional requirement that the constituent states of our federation reciprocate recognition of each other's laws. See Ross, *Has the Conflict of Laws Become a Branch of Constitutional Law?* (1931) 15 MINN. L. REV. 161.

[60] Colorado v. Harbeck, 232 N. Y. 71, 133 N. E. 357 (1921); Moore v. Mitchell, 28 F.(2d) 997 (S. D. N. Y. 1928), 30 F.(2d) 600 (C. C. A. 2d, 1929). See also Note, *Extra-Territorial Collection of State Inheritance Taxes* (1929) 29 COLUMBIA LAW REV. 782.

all states must accord it full faith and credit.[61] And if, as has been indicated, administrative determinations are entitled to the same standing as judgments,[62] the way is open for each state to project its revenue acts into all other states to some considerable degree. Of course, if a tax assessment were treated like a judgment, jurisdiction would be open to inquiry. But for reasons which do not seem entirely convincing to me the federal courts have been pretty effectually closed to the aggrieved taxpayer who seeks a determination as to which of the state taxing statutes rightly applies to him or to his estate.[63] We are close to holding that any tax a state has physical power to collect it has the constitutional right to keep.

Another class of cases in which the faith and credit clause has been invoked involves overlapping

[61] Milwaukee County v. M. E. White Co., 296 U. S. 268 (1935).
[62] Magnolia Petroleum Co. v. Hunt, 320 U. S. 430 (1943); cf. Broderick v. Rosner, 294 U. S. 629 (1935).
[63] Dorrance v. Pennsylvania, 287 U. S. 660 (1932) and 288 U. S. 617 (1933) (cert. denied to review Dorrance's Estate, 309 Pa. 151); Dorrance v. Martin, 298 U. S. 678 (1936) (cert. denied to review Dorrance v. Thayer-Martin, 116 N. J. L. 362); Hill v. Martin, 296 U. S. 393 (1935). See also Worcester County Trust Co. v. Riley, 302 U. S. 292 (1937); New Jersey v. Pennsylvania, 287 U. S. 580 (1933); Massachusetts v. Missouri, 308 U. S. 1 (1939); Texas v. Florida, 306 U. S. 398 (1939); State Tax Commission v. Aldrich, 316 U. S. 174 (1942); International Harvester Co. v. Wisconsin Dept. of Taxation, 322 U. S. 435 (1944); General Trading Co. v. Tax Commission, 322 U. S. 335 (1944); Northwest Airlines, Inc. v. Minnesota, 322 U. S. 292 (1944); see Sargent and Tweed, *Death and Taxes Are Certain—but What of Domicile* (1939) 53 HARV. L. REV. 68.

[27]

workmen's compensation statutes. They have called forth the Court's most elaborate efforts to explain and rationalize its choice of law under the faith and credit clause. The Court has said that it will choose which of two contending state statutes shall apply to a controversy by appraising the governmental interests of each jurisdiction and turning the scale of decision according to their weights. The forum *prima facie*, of course, is entitled to apply its own law. "One who challenges that right, because of the force given to a conflicting statute of another state by the full faith and credit clause, assumes the burden of showing, upon some rational basis, that of the conflicting interests involved those of the foreign state are superior to those of the forum." [64]

The practical results of such standards appear in three workmen's compensation cases. In the first, the interest of the forum state was held to be "only casual," although it was the state in which a workman on public utility lines was killed. The state where he lived and was hired was held to have a superior interest which ousted the law of the forum.[65] Soon thereafter it was held that a forum state, being the place of hiring, but not of claimant's domicile, could apply its own law to compensate for an accident elsewhere, since "no persuasive reason is

[64] Alaska Packers Ass'n. v. Industrial Accident Comm'n, 294 U. S. 532, 547–48 (1935).
[65] Bradford Electric Light Co. v. Clapper, 286 U. S. 145 (1932) (opinion by Mr. Justice Brandeis).

[28]

shown for denying" that right in favor of the law of the place of accident.[66] Somewhat later the Court held, however, that the state of accident may apply its own compensation laws and need not give faith and credit to those of a state that was the place of hiring and the domicile of both the employer and the employee.[67] But a forum state may no longer apply its laws if an award under other state law has been made.[68]

Nowhere has the Court attempted, although faith and credit opinions have been written by some of its boldest-thinking and clearest-speaking Justices, to define standards by which "superior state interests" in the subject matter of conflicting statutes are to be weighed. Nor can I discern any consistent pattern or design into which the cases fit.

Indeed, I think it difficult to point to any field in which the Court has more completely demonstrated or more candidly confessed the lack of guiding standards of a legal character than in trying to determine what choice of law is required by the Constitution.

[66] Alaska Packers Ass'n. v. Industrial Accident Comm'n, 294 U. S. 532 (1935).
[67] Pacific Employers Ins. Co. v. Industrial Accident Comm'n, 306 U. S. 493 (1939).
[68] Magnolia Petroleum Co. v. Hunt, 320 U. S. 430 (1943); see Cheatham, *Res Judicata and the Full Faith and Credit Clause* (1944) 44 COLUMBIA LAW REV. 330.

HAVE STATUTORY AND DECISIONAL LAW UNDER THIS CLAUSE MET THE NEEDS OF OUR SOCIETY?

By other articles of the Constitution our forefathers created a political union among otherwise independent and sovereign states. By other provisions too, they sought to integrate the economic life of the country. By the full faith and credit clause they sought to federalize the separate and independent state legal systems by the overriding principle of reciprocal recognition of public acts, records, and judicial proceedings. It was placed foremost among those measures [69] which would guard the new political and economic union against the disintegrating influence of provincialism in jurisprudence, but without aggrandizement of federal power at the expense of the states.

Manifestly the evils of usurpation feared by Randolph have not been experienced—at least not from this clause. The states themselves have sought in general to attain a greater measure of uniformity

---

[69] It was followed by the provision to a similar purpose that "The Citizens of each State shall be entitled to all Privileges and Immunities of Citizens in the several States." U. S. CONST., Art. IV, § 2, Cl. 1. This, too, came from the Articles of Confederation, which provided that "the free inhabitants of each of these States . . . shall be entitled to all privileges and immunities of free citizens in the several States; and the people of each State shall have free ingress and regress to and from any other State, and shall enjoy therein all the privileges of trade and commerce, subject to the same duties, impositions and restrictions as the inhabitants thereof respectively. . . ." ARTICLES OF CONFEDERATION, Art. IV.

in private law than Congress or the federal courts have sought to impose.[70] Their judiciaries have voluntarily accepted as part of their own common law the principles of Conflict of Laws. Judge Cardozo, writing for the New York Court of Appeals, said, and with good reason, "There is a growing conviction that only exceptional circumstances should lead one of the states to refuse to enforce a right acquired in another. The evidences of this tendency are many." [71] Whether it is because of outmoded ideas of comity, or because of a disposition to protect rights thought to have vested elsewhere, or simply because it is thought a wise local policy in administering justice,[72] our state courts are generally hospitable to pleas that public acts or decisions of another state be taken into account. Generosity in applying foreign law no doubt has forestalled pursuit of many questions as constitutional ones under the full faith and credit clause.

To a foreign observer the United States may well

[70] The state legislatures have generally supported the work of the Commission on Uniform Laws and often have adopted its proposals. State judges, among whom Judge Cardozo led, supported the Restatements of the common law by the American Law Institute.

[71] Loucks v. Standard Oil Co., 224 N. Y. 99, 113, 120 N. E. 198, 202 (1918); see Graybar Electric Co. v. New Amsterdam Casualty Co., 292 N. Y. 246, 54 N. E.(2d) 811, 813 (1944), *cert. denied* Oct. 9, 1944.

[72] These different theoretical bases are interestingly discussed by Dodd, *The Power of the Supreme Court to Review State Decisions in the Field of Conflict of Laws* (1926) 39 HARV. L. REV. 533. Judge Cardozo did not think highly of the comity theory and leaned toward the theory of vested rights. See Loucks v. Standard Oil Co., 224 N. Y. 99, 110, 120 N. E. 198, 201 (1918).

appear to be "a nation concealed under the form of a federation." [73] However true this may be as to political power and economic controls, it is far wide of the truth as to administration of internal justice among our forty-eight state legal systems. Indeed, today in respect of our legal administrations we have not achieved a much "more perfect union" than that of the colonies under the Articles of Confederation. We have so far as I can ascertain the most localized and conflicting system of any country which presents the external appearance of nationhood. But we are so accustomed to the delays, expense, and frustrations of our system that it seldom occurs to us to inquire whether these are wise or constitutionally necessary. Perhaps the best perspective for judging whether our society is being well served by its present legislative and decisional law under the faith and credit clause is by comparative study of the methods and degree of integration employed by other peoples whose heritage and jurisprudence are comparable to our own.[74]

Great Britain, since 1801, has successfully employed a system of reciprocal registration and execution of judgments. It began between only England and Ireland.[75] In 1868 it was extended to include the

---

[73] DICEY, LAW OF THE CONSTITUTION (9th ed. 1939) Appendix, p. 604, which was in 1915 edition.

[74] Switzerland may not be considered comparable. But see Schoch, *Conflict of Laws in a Federal State: The Experience of Switzerland* (1942) 55 HARV. L. REV. 738.

[75] Crown Debts Act, 1801, 41 GEO. III, c. 90, §§ 5, 6.

[32]

whole United Kingdom,[76] and in 1920 Parliament made provision for bringing the entire British Empire under a system of reciprocal enforcement of judgments.[77] England also, in actions considered appropriate, permits jurisdiction of the person to be obtained by service of process out of the territorial jurisdiction of the Court.[78]

Perhaps the most instructive comparisons are with

[76] The Judgments Extension Act, 1868, 31 & 32 VICT., c. 54; Inferior Courts Judgments Extension Act, 1882, 45 & 46 VICT., c. 31.
[77] Administration of Justice Act, 1920, 10 & 11 GEO. V, c. 81, Part II. It has been extended by Orders in Council to a large part of the Empire. See 6 HALSBURY, LAWS OF ENGLAND (2d ed. 1932) 348, n. (d). See Piggott, *The Execution of British and Colonial Judgments within the Dominions* (1922) 38 L. Q. REV. 339.
[78] It is provided that jurisdiction may be obtained, in the High Court, by service out of the jurisdiction at the discretion of the Court:

(1) When the whole subject-matter of the action is land situate within the jurisdiction or the perpetuation of testimony relating to the title to such land.

(2) When any act, deed, will, contract, obligation or liability affecting land or hereditaments within the jurisdiction is sought to be construed, rectified, set aside, or enforced in the action.

(3) When any relief is sought against any person domiciled or ordinarily resident within the jurisdiction.

(4) When the action is for the administration of the personal estate of any deceased person domiciled within the jurisdiction at the time of his death, or for the execution, as to property within the jurisdiction, of the trusts of any written instrument of which the person to be served is trustee, and which ought to be executed according to the law of England.

(5) When the action is brought against a defendant not domiciled or ordinarily resident in Scotland, to enforce, rescind, dissolve, annul, or otherwise affect a contract or to recover damages for breach of a contract made within the jurisdiction, or made by an agent trading or residing within the jurisdiction, on behalf of a principal outside the jurisdiction, or which by its terms or by implication is governed by English law.

(6) When the action is brought against a defendant not domiciled or ordinarily resident in Scotland or Ireland in respect of a

[33]

the two English-speaking federations, Canada and Australia. Canada federated under the Dominion Government in 1867, and the Australian states federated under the Commonwealth in 1900. Both fundamental acts were framed after careful and critical studies of our constitutional practice, and their departures from it represent a judgment upon our weaknesses and defects pronounced by people of purpose and traditions much like our own.[79] Both of them concentrated in federal control many heads of

---

breach, committed within the jurisdiction, of a contract, wherever made.

(7) When the action is founded on a tort committed within the jurisdiction.

(8) When any injunction is sought as to anything to be done within the jurisdiction, or any nuisance within the jurisdiction is sought to be prevented or removed.

(9) When any person out of the jurisdiction is a necessary or proper party to an action properly brought against some other person served within the jurisdiction.

(10) When the action relates to a mortgage of personal property located within the jurisdiction.

(11) When the action is under the Carriage by Air Act, R. S. C. Ord. 11, r. 1; 26 HALSBURY, LAWS OF ENGLAND (2d ed. 1937) 31.

[79] In a speech to the Canadian Parliament in August of 1865, Sir John Macdonald said, "Ever since the [American] Union was formed the difficulty of what is called 'state rights' has existed, and this has had much to do in bringing up the present unhappy war in the United States . . . we have adopted a different system. We have strengthened the general government. We have given the general legislature all the great subjects of legislation. We have conferred on them, not only specifically and in detail all the powers which are incident to sovereignty, but we have expressly declared that all subjects of general interest not distinctly and exclusively conferred upon the local governments and local legislatures, shall be conferred upon the general government and legislature. We have thus avoided that great source of weakness which has been the cause of disruption in the United States." Quoted in Proceedings Special Committee on B. N. A. Act, Canadian House of Commons, Session of 1935, p. 81.

private law which among us are left to the states and, of course, generate conflicts.[80] The interpretative process, moreover, in both countries, is integrated to a degree which makes conflict much less likely to occur. Canadian judges, of provincial as well as of dominion courts, are appointed by the Crown on motion of the Dominion Government, and there are no separate federal courts of first instance. Thus, both provincial and federal law are applied by a single system of courts. Australia, while retaining the preexisting separate judicial systems of the several states, has a single national high court of general appeal from the state courts in all cases and in all fields.[81]

Canada does without a full faith and credit clause, no doubt finding the principles of private international law as to statutes and *res judicata* doctrine as to judgments adequate in its highly unified judicial system. Australia substantially copied our faith and credit clause, except that Parliament was specifically empowered to legislate with respect to "the service

---

[80] Our Constitution federalizes power over eighteen enumerated subjects; Canada, over twenty-nine; and Australia, over thirty-nine. Canada vests the residual powers in the Dominion as well as express powers over such subjects as bills of exchange and promissory notes, interest, banking, marriage and divorce. See British North America Act, 1867, 30 & 31 VICT., c. 3, § 91. Australia adds such subjects as insurance, trading and financial corporations, all foreign corporations, telephonic, telegraphic, and like services. CONSTITUTION OF AUSTRALIA, § 51.

[81] British North America Act, Art. VII; CONSTITUTION OF AUSTRALIA, Ch. III; 1 BRYCE, STUDIES IN HISTORY AND JURISPRUDENCE (1901) 416.

and execution throughout the Commonwealth of the civil and criminal process and the judgments of the courts of the States." [82] Parliament promptly exercised these powers. With provisions to safeguard against abuse and injustice, process of state courts in appropriate classes of cases is authorized to be served anywhere in Australia, and their judgments may upon registration be executed in any state.[83]

Thus, if we look about us, we see that peoples who, no less than we, love local independence and home rule have in the nineteenth and twentieth centuries got away from the sharp territorial delimitations on court process which prevailed in the eighteenth. Both process to initiate and process to terminate actions are regulated, not by the accidents of geography, but by the appropriateness of a particular venue in which to commence an action and by universal respect for the judgment which settles it. We alone in a century and a half have made no effort better to integrate our judicial systems. These confining concepts, which do so much to make our judgments ineffective or to delay and increase the costs of their execution and do so much to complicate our choice of law problems, present a challenge to our times and most of all to our profession.

[82] CONSTITUTION OF AUSTRALIA, §§ 118, 51 (xxiv), (xxv).
[83] Service and Execution of Process Act 1901–1934, 2 COMMONWEALTH ACTS, 1901–1935 (1936) 1415.

LEGISLATIVE POWER BETTER TO INTEGRATE OUR LEGAL SYSTEMS

Any such complete integration of our separate legal systems through compulsory reciprocal recognition of process and execution of judgments, of course, is beyond the judicial power of innovation. But it cannot be doubted that Congress is invested with a range of power greatly exceeding that which it has seen fit to exercise. It may aid our perspective to review some of the proposals for legislation looking in that direction.

First of all are the suggestions to simplify the execution of state judgments. Madison, you will recall, wished for legislative power to provide for the execution of judgments in other states under such regulations as might be expedient. He thought that this might be safely done and was justified by the nature of the Union. In 1927 a committee of distinguished lawyers made an exceptionally able report to the American Bar Association including a proposed bill to carry out Madison's idea, and the Association recommended its adoption by Congress.[84] The reform seems to have died a-borning.

---

[84] Mr. Henry W. Taft was chairman of the committee, which among others included James M. Beck, Roscoe Pound, William L. Ransom, Edson R. Sunderland, George E. Beers, Jefferson P. Chandler, and Stephen H. Allen. *Report of the Standing Committee on Jurisprudence and Law Reform*, 52 A. B. A. REP. (1927) 292. Adopted: Proceedings, *id.* at 81. See also Corwin, *The "Full Faith and Credit" Clause* (1933) 81 U. OF PA. L. REV. 371; COOK, THE LOGICAL AND LEGAL BASES OF THE CONFLICT OF LAWS (1942) 90.

[37]

Other suggestions have been made to reach particular evils. Mr. Justice Stone, joined by Mr. Justice Cardozo, pointed out in a dissenting opinion that "Much of the confusion and procedural deficiencies" in the matrimonial field might be remedied by legislation.[85] It is also suggested that Congress has power to prescribe the type of divorce judgment that is entitled to extraterritorial recognition.[86] The Court has had no occasion to decide such questions, but I should say it has been fairly ostentatious in leaving the way open to sustain such enactments without embarrassment.[87]

Congress, however, not only has failed to provide for nationwide enforcement of judgments of state courts, but it has affirmatively subjected the effectiveness of judgments of federal courts to like territorial limitations.[88] The fact is that today, except in the few

[85] Yarborough v. Yarborough, 290 U. S. 202, 215, n. 2 (1933) (dissent).
[86] Corwin, *The "Full Faith and Credit Clause," supra* note 84, at 388.
[87] *Cf.* Williams v. North Carolina, 317 U. S. 287 (1942).
[88] Congress has never provided a general federal procedure to execute judgments and to regulate liens, exemptions, levies, sales, garnishment and supplementary proceedings. Instead, the Process Act of 1789 adopted the common-law remedies on judgments provided by the law of the state in which the federal court was held. See 28 U. S. C. § 727 (1940); Warren, *Federal Process and State Legislation* (1930) 16 VA. L. REV. 421. It came to be assumed, although Congress had not expressly said so, that federal executions were thereby subject to the same territorial limitations as state executions. United States v. Morris, 10 Wheat. 246, 281 (U. S. 1825); Toland v. Sprague, 12 Pet. 300, 328 (U. S. 1838). Execution may run into another district of the same state, 36 STAT. 1167 (1911), 28 U. S. C. § 838 (1940), and on a judgment in favor of the United States may run anywhere, 28 U. S. C. § 839 (1940). The new Federal

[38]

cases of which the United States Supreme Court has original jurisdiction, the litigant can go into no court of the land whose judgment will have any effect outside a very limited area except as a record on which to sue for another judgment. If such parochial limitations serve any good purpose in modern society, I do not know what they are.

Of course, process instituting an action should be governed by very different considerations than process to execute a final judgment. While no one should avoid or escape from a final judgment rendered by a court having jurisdiction, there are relatively few circumstances under which one should be summoned to trial outside his home district or state. But one is put to it to find any answer to the suggestion that the power of Congress is ample to require in appropriate cases recognition of state court civil process served anywhere in the United States.[89] Such legislation might encounter due process, or perhaps other constitutional objections, if it attempted to transport trials to places unrelated to the parties or events.[90]

Rules of Civil Procedure perpetuate this pattern. Rule 69. Is it not time that we stop thinking that, because for administrative purposes it is convenient to divide the United States into judicial districts, a federal court only "sits within and for that district; and is bounded by its local limits," as the Supreme Court once put it? (Toland v. Sprague, 12 Pet. 300, 328 [U. S. 1838]). It also sits within and for the United States, and why should its judgments not be judgments everywhere?

[89] See COOK, THE LOGICAL AND LEGAL BASES OF THE CONFLICT OF LAWS (1942) 99–100.

[90] *Cf.* Davis v. Farmers Co-operative Equity Co., 262 U. S. 312 (1923), where the commerce clause prevented trial in Minnesota of case between strangers on imported cause of action.

[39]

But within the ambit of reasonable judicial administration it would seem hard to construe the power to prescribe the extraterritorial effect of "judicial proceedings" otherwise than as comprehending power to prescribe the effect of proceedings which initiate, as well as of those that terminate, litigation.[91]

But here, again, Congress, instead of using its powers to integrate the legal systems of the states, has impressed the state limitations upon the federal courts. Beginning over a century ago, the Supreme Court repeatedly has reminded that "Congress might have authorized civil process from any circuit [now district] court, to have run into any state of the Union. It has not done so." [92] Nor has it done so yet, apart from exceptional cases.[93]

[91] *Cf.*, however, Barber v. Barber, No. 51, Oct. Term 1944, decided Dec. 4, 1944.
[92] Toland v. Sprague, 12 Pet. 300, 328 (U. S. 1838); United States v. Union Pacific R. R., 98 U. S. 569, 604 (1878); Robertson v. Railroad Labor Board, 268 U. S. 619, 622 (1925). In the latter case Mr. Justice Brandeis gives an exhaustive review of statutory and decisional law bearing on this subject in the course of an opinion refusing, quite properly, I think, to extend a statute by implication so as to give a governmental agency a right to sue an individual in a district where he neither was found for service nor was an inhabitant.
[93] General provisions are found in Judicial Code §§ 54, 55, 56, 57, 58; 36 STAT. 1102 (1911), 28 U. S. C. §§ 115, 116, 117, 118, 119 (1940). Exceptions are such as interpleader in veterans' insurance cases, 38 U. S. C. § 445 (1940); interpleader, 49 STAT. 1096 (1936), 28 U. S. C. § 41 (26) (c) (1940); suits to restrain violations of the antitrust acts, 26 STAT. 210 (1890), 28 STAT. 570 (1894), 38 STAT. 736 (1914), 15 U. S. C. §§ 5, 10, 25; railroad and corporate reorganizations, 53 STAT. 1406 (1939), 52 STAT. 884 (1938), 11 U. S. C. §§ 205 (a), 511; see Continental Illinois Nat. Bank & Trust Co. v. Chicago, R. I. & P. Ry., 294 U. S. 648, 682 (1935); *In re* Greyling Reality Corp., 74 F.(2d) 734 (C. C. A. 2d 1935). The

Thus, when one must seek a remedy, whether he turns to state courts or to federal courts, he finds them subject to territorial limitations which often force one injured in person or property to go far from the place of all the transactions and away from the only place he ever has lived or traded, to some distant forum.[94] But apart from the convenience of litigants, it is in the public interest that trials be held in appropriate places. And if transactions are litigated where they took place, it usually means that the forum can apply its own law to the case. To hear the case elsewhere often raises the choice of law issue which so besets our courts. I think it is more than a coincidence that nowhere else in the modern world is judicial authority so dispersed among disjointed and insular units, nowhere else is the choice of place of trial so much regulated as a by-product of territorial limits on jurisdiction, and nowhere else does

---

Federal Rules of Civil Procedure perpetuate the territorial limitations on service of process of federal courts. Rule 4(f).

[94] The problem of securing justice at home against foreign corporations who are present for trading purposes but are not to be "found" for service of process is a serious one. See Rosenberg Bros. & Co. v. Curtis Brown Co., 260 U. S. 516 (1923); James-Dickinson Farm Mortgage Co. v. Harry, 273 U. S. 119 (1927). These cases pushed due process protection for foreign corporations beyond that which our New York courts thought required or desirable. See National Furniture Co. v. Spiegelman & Co., 198 App. Div. 672, 190 N. Y. Supp. 831 (4th Dept. 1921); Fleischmann Construction Co. v. Blauner's, 190 App. Div. 95, 179 N. Y. Supp. 193 (1st Dept. 1919). And see opinion of Hiscock, C. J., in The Robert Dollar Co. v. Canadian Car & Foundry Co., 220 N. Y. 270, 115 N. E. 711 (1917). Years ago I declaimed with some heat against this trend. *What Price "Due Process"* (1927) 5 N. Y. L. REV. 435.

[41]

litigation present such a multitude and complexity of controversies over conflict of laws.

Of course, the reasons for this system lie deep in our history. No one would wish to impair the traditional separateness and independence of the judicial systems of the several states. But to implement their jurisdictions in proper cases by requiring reciprocal recognition of process and to regulate interstate venue somewhat as New York regulates venue within the state [95] could hardly be thought to invade the power reserved to the states. It is not suggested, of course, that either a state or a federal court be authorized to call one to a foreign state to answer complaints except where some circumstance makes trial more just and appropriate there than elsewhere. But in that class of cases I see no reason why fortuitous circumstances concerning service of process should preclude an intelligent determination of venue.

But the calendars of successive sessions of Congress are crowded with proposals of more immediate

[95] New York's highest court of original jurisdiction sits in and for the several counties, but its process runs throughout the state. But venue is fixed in some classes of cases by residence of the parties, in others by the location of property which is the subject of the action, and in others by the place where the cause of action arose. All of this is topped off with a grant of wide discretion to the court to change place of trial where the plaintiff designates an improper county, where an impartial trial cannot be had there, or where the convenience of witnesses and the ends of justice require trial elsewhere. CIVIL PRACTICE ACT, Art. 23, §§ 182=187 and Art. 25, § 225. See discussion of problems of jurisdiction and venue in Foster, *Place of Trial in Civil Actions* (1930) 43 HARV. L. REV. 1217; Foster, *Place of Trial—Interstate Application of Intrastate Methods of Adjustment* (1930) 44 HARV. L. REV. 41.

[42]

urgency, supported by pressures greater than usually can be mustered for a law reform. I suspect the judiciary will long be left to struggle with these conditions without aid of legislation, and to the judicial problems we will return.

THE QUEST FOR PRINCIPLES OF EXTRATERRITORIAL FAITH AND CREDIT FOR STATE LAW

I suppose most judges, like Judge Cardozo, would be glad to leave all creation of new law to statutes if only they gave promise of being adequate to the burden.[96] But courts cannot, like legislatures, choose their time to act. The turbulent life about us throws up new kinds of cases which we must promptly decide. They push us into choosing between competing principles. Where there is a choice under the full faith and credit clause, the one should be made, I should say, which best will meet the needs of an expanding national society for a modern system of administering, inexpensively and expeditiously, a more certain justice. Of course, the choice must be kept within the traditional limitations on the interpretative process. But these great constitutional generalities, as Judge Cardozo said, "have a content and a significance that vary from age to age," and judges must not stop at mere "ascertainment of the meaning and intent of lawmakers"; their interpretation "supplements the declaration" and "fills the vacant

[96] CARDOZO, THE GROWTH OF THE LAW 132.

[43]

spaces." [97] Accordingly, he took "judge-made law as one of the existing realities of life" [98] and maintained that the judicial process in its "highest reaches is not discovery, but creation." [99]

But these were sober counsels addressed to sober men. That they would not always be so read, he knew. He warned against mere improvisation, undisciplined by the hard work of our craft, based on "sentiment or benevolence or some vague notion of social welfare." [100] In his last lecture—to me one of the most significant—he told us that it is a "misleading cult" which teaches "that the remedy for our ills is to have the law give over, once and for all, the strivings of the centuries for a rational coherence, and sink back in utter weariness to a justice that is the flickering reflection of the impulse of the moment." [101]

Which among the values that Judge Cardozo thought should enter into the calculus of decision should predominate when we deal with faith and credit? This seems to be a field of law which calls "in conspicuous measure for certainty and order, for an administration of justice that is strict and in a sense mechanical." [102] What he said of the Conflict of Laws seems applicable: "We deal there with the ap-

[97] CARDOZO, THE NATURE OF THE JUDICIAL PROCESS 17.
[98] *Id.* at 10.   [99] *Id.* at 166; THE GROWTH OF THE LAW 57.
[100] THE GROWTH OF THE LAW 59–60.
[101] Cardozo, *The Judicial Process up to Now*, 55 REPORTS N. Y. STATE BAR ASS'N (1932) 271.
[102] THE GROWTH OF THE LAW 81–82.

[44]

plication of law in space. The walls of the compartments must be firm, the lines of demarcation plain, or there will be overlappings and encroachments with incongruities and clashes. In such circumstances, the finality of the rule is in itself a jural end." [103] The faith and credit clause would not seem to lend itself to sociological, ethical, or economic ends or implications, except that "certainty and order are themselves constituents of the welfare which it is our business to discover." [104] And of course, "One of the most fundamental social interests is that law shall be uniform and impartial. There must be nothing in its action that savors of prejudice or favor or even arbitrary whim or fitfulness." [105] "It will not do to decide the same question one way between one set of litigants and the opposite way between another. . . . 'If a case was decided against me yesterday when I was defendant, I shall look for the same judgment today if I am plaintiff.' . . . Adherence to precedent must then be the rule rather than the exception if litigants are to have faith in the even-handed administration of justice in the courts." [106]

In the century and a half of the Court's existence, litigation as to faith and credit chiefly has concerned

[103] CARDOZO, THE PARADOXES OF LEGAL SCIENCE 67.
[104] THE GROWTH OF THE LAW 79; THE NATURE OF THE JUDICIAL PROCESS 67.
[105] THE NATURE OF THE JUDICIAL PROCESS 112.
[106] *Id.* at 33–34, in part quoting MILLER, THE DATA OF JURISPRUDENCE (1903) 335.

[45]

the recognition due to judgments. In this field the Court has built up a body of law. I do not think it departs essentially from the principles of the clause, even though it may leave it somewhat short of faultless fulfillment. While Judge Cardozo pointed out with great accuracy that the power of the precedent is only "the power of the beaten track," [107] still the mere fact that a path is a beaten one is a persuasive reason for following it. This is especially true in this class of cases, where the doctrine must in the first instance be applied chiefly in our many state courts. To be administered uniformly a rule of faith and credit must be relatively stable, certain, and of long standing.

But precedent does not offer any such well-beaten path to show when a forum must accord faith and credit to the statutory and decisional law of another state. Decisions are less numerous and less consistent. As legislation becomes more complex and enters new spheres, conflicts in this field grow in number and importance. Here it is that the creative intelligence of the judicial process seems to meet its greatest challenge under the faith and credit clause. It would not be fitting to suggest how I might think particular cases should be resolved. But it has not seemed inappropriate to state some views as to the general philosophy of decision if our own time is to utilize this clause to realize its purpose as a principle of order in our federated legal systems.

[107] CARDOZO, THE GROWTH OF THE LAW 62.

That the Supreme Court should impose uniformity in choice-of-law problems is a prospect comforting to none, least of all to a member of that body. I have not paid any exaggerated tribute to its performance thus far in this complex field. But the available courses from which our choice may be made seem to me limited. One is for us to leave choice of law in all cases to the local policy of the state. This seems to me to be at odds with the implication of our federal system that the mutual limits of the states' powers are defined by the Constitution. It also seems productive of confusion, for it means that choice among conflicting substantive rules depends only upon which state happens to have the last word. And that we are not likely to accept such a principle is certainly indicated by the Court's sporadic interferences with choice of law, whether under the rubric of due process, full faith and credit, or otherwise.[108] A second course is for us to adopt no rule, permit a good deal of overlapping and confusion, but interfere now and then without imparting to the bar any reason by which the one or the other course is to be guided or predicted. This seems to me about where our present decisions leave us. Third, we may candidly recognize that choice-of-law questions, when properly raised, ought to and do present constitutional questions under the full faith and credit clause [109] which the Court may properly decide and as to which it

---

[108] See notes 45, 55, 58, 64, 65, *supra*.
[109] Or, in some cases, perhaps, under the due process clause.

ought at least to mark out reasonably narrow limits of permissible variation in areas where there is confusion.

Always to be kept in mind in dealing with these problems is that the policy ultimately to be served in application of the clause is the federal policy of "a more perfect union" of our legal systems. No local interest and no balance of local interests can rise above this consideration. It is hard to see how the faith and credit clause would have any practical meaning as to statutes if the Court should adhere to the statement that "a state is not required to enforce a law obnoxious to its public policy." [110]

The distinction between federal interest and local interest may be elusive, but always it is present in these conflicts. Fundamental to every such conflict of law is that separate states consider that their own interests require inconsistent social or economic policies. The legal controversy as to whether Dred Scott's sojourn in a free state invested him with rights which must be respected when he returned to a slave state had its roots in the two incompatible social systems. Conflicts which we face day after day are less deep and less bitter, but nonetheless they grow out of disagreement between states as to the policies that will promote their social welfare. One state thinks it needs to encourage industrial capital to come and exploit its latent resources and therefore is niggardly about putting the burden of industrial ac-

[110] Griffin v. McCoach, 313 U. S. 498, 507 (1941) ; see *supra*, note 51.

cidents upon industry. Another, more fully industrialized, perhaps, adopts a policy of more generous workmen's compensation. Or religious convictions prevailing in one state may lead to a highly restrictive policy of divorce, while another grants it on easy terms. Or one state finds actions for alienation of affections or for breach of promise to be productive of more evil than good and abolishes such causes of action; other nearby states adhere to the policy of permitting recovery. Or the state where a man dies declares him domiciled therein and exercises its right to administer his estate. Several other states make claims based on assessment procedures, for which they demand faith and credit. The state where the decedent had a summer home and the one where he spent his winters both declare themselves to be the state of domicile; another claims on the ground that it is the place where certain evidences of intangible property are deposited for safekeeping; various others, because the intangibles were shares in or obligations of corporations which they had chartered; while still others file claims showing that the issuing companies did business within their borders and that some part of the value transferred was created in such state.[111] Now, of course, there is no federal power over these matters, and there is no constitutional policy that one should or should not recover for alienation of affections, or be subject to

[111] Each such basis has been held permissible. See cases cited in note 63, *supra*.

strict or easy rules of divorce, or that an injured workman should proceed under one compensation system rather than another or under common law, nor is there a federal policy that one should or should not pay a particular state tax.

Certainly the personal preferences of the Justices among the conflicting state policies is not a permissible basis of determining which shall prevail in a case. But only a singularly balanced mind could weigh relative state interests in such subject matter except by resort to what are likely to be strong preferences in sociology, economics, governmental theory, and politics. There are no judicial standards of valuation of such imponderables. How can we know which is the greater interest when one state is moved by one set of considerations—economic, perhaps—to one policy, and another by different considerations—social welfare, perhaps—to a conflicting one? But, even if we could appraise or compare relative local interests, we must lift these questions above the control of local interest and must govern conflict in these cases by the wider considerations arising out of the federal order. How to determine when these require the law of the forum to give way to that of another state seems to me an unsettled question. I cannot regard the "balance of interest" test used in the compensation cases as more than a tentative and inadequate answer. It seems to assume that a state must have power to reach a matter because it has an interest in it—a power which yields only to a greater power based on a greater interest. I doubt that the position can long be maintained that the reach of a state's power is a by-product of an interest. The ultimate answer, it seems to me, will have to be based on considerations of state relations to each other and to the federal system. What is the basis of power in a constituent state of our Federation to govern a controversy, when is it exclusive of a like power asserted for another state on the same or some different basis, and when is it entitled to prevail even in the forums of another state? I leave you pretty much at large on this subject, for that is where the decisions leave me. But I could suggest no more engaging intellectual enterprise to which the scholarship of our profession might turn than to try to find the wise answers on constitutional grounds to these questions.

Even when each conflicting policy claims recognition on the same ground and the conflict proceeds from contrary findings of fact, there would seem to be a federal interest, distinct from that of either state, in its solution. Domicile is the ground which furnishes the best example. The Supreme Court still adheres, as I think it must long continue to do, to the doctrine that a domiciliary relationship of a party to the state is a sufficient basis to support various exercises of state power.[112] But the Court has said that "Neither the Fourteenth Amendment nor the full faith and credit clause requires uniformity in the de-

---

[112] *E.g.*, Skiriotes v. Florida, 313 U. S. 69 (1941) (criminal acts on high seas); Milliken v. Meyer, 311 U. S. 457 (1940) (extraterritorial

[51]

cisions of the courts of different states as to the place of domicile, where the exertion of state power is dependent upon domicile within its boundaries." [113] This seems to me to beg the real question which seeks federal decision. The real issue is not whether the court of either state must conform its decision to that of the other, but whether both must conform their decisions in this field to some federal constitutional standard.

Of course, the federal courts do not, by reason of the full faith and credit clause, have any federal interest to consider as to which of two disputed places is one's correct domicile. The Constitution is indifferent as to whether a Mr. Williams was domiciled in North Carolina or in Nevada or whether a Mr. Green was domiciled in New York, Massachusetts, or Texas. But I do think that the federal interest is concerned that a Mr. Williams and a Mr. Green have some place in our federal system where they really belong for purposes of fixing their legal status and determining by whom they shall be governed. Such a view certainly is consistent with the spirit and, perhaps, is required by the implications of the Fourteenth Amendment, which provides, "All persons born or naturalized in the United States, and subject to the jurisdiction thereof, are citizens of the United

---

service of process); Lawrence v. State Tax Commission, 286 U. S. 276 (1932); New York *ex rel.* Cohn v. Graves, 300 U. S. 308 (1937) (taxation); Williams v. North Carolina, 317 U. S. 287 (1942) (judgment of divorce).

[113] Worcester County Trust Co. v. Riley, 302 U. S. 292, 299 (1937).

[52]

States and *of the State wherein they* reside [italics supplied]." This provision would seem to do something toward fixing one's place in our federal society. It seems to fix one standard by which to know where political rights and obligations are to be determined. Where the requisite relationship between person and place exists to warrant state exercise of power and to exclude other states from a conflicting exercise of power would seem to present, at least in connection with a faith and credit problem, a federal question on which, when properly raised, litigants would be entitled to the judgment of a federal court.

In considering claims of foreign law for faith and credit, courts, of course, find conflict of laws a relevant and enlightening body of experience and authority to provide analogies. But while the American law of conflicts is a somewhat parallel and contemporaneous development with the law of faith and credit, they are also quite independent evolutions, are based on contrary basic assumptions, and at times support conflicting results. We must beware of transposing conflicts doctrines into the law of the Constitution. This is exactly what appears, from the opinions, to have been done in several of the cases where exceptions were made as to faith and credit due judgments.[114] Private international law and the law of conflicts extend recognition to foreign statutes or judgments by rules developed by a free forum as

[114] *E.g.*, M'Elmoyle v. Cohen, 13 Pet. 312 (U. S. 1839); Wisconsin v. Pelican Ins. Co., 127 U. S. 265 (1888).

[53]

a matter of enlightened self-interest. The constitutional provision extends recognition on the basis of the interests of the federal union, which supersedes freedom of individual state action by a compulsory policy of reciprocal rights to demand and obligations to render faith and credit. States, under their voluntary policy, may extend recognition when they could not constitutionally be required to do so; and sometimes, of course, they have interpreted the law of conflicts to refuse credit when the constitutional mandate is held to require it.

Occasions which require the forum to make a choice between application of its own law and that of some other state would be less frequent if courts were free to decline cases that might more appropriately be litigated elsewhere and also if appropriate courts were enabled better to get jurisdiction of the persons concerned.[115] In both these respects decisions of the Supreme Court, chiefly under the due process clause, have shown a pretty consistent and long-sustained trend toward extending both state freedom to decline and state power to acquire jurisdiction.

Mr. Justice Cardozo, in 1932, was the first Justice, I believe, to have the hardihood to refer in a Supreme Court opinion to the doctrine of *forum non conveniens* by name.[116] But the idea that a court has inherent discretion to decline a cause otherwise within

[115] See *supra*, pp. 40–41.
[116] Rogers v. Guaranty Trust Co., 288 U. S. 123, 151 (1933). See, on the subject of *forum non conveniens*, Blair, *The Doctrine of Forum*

its jurisdiction which is more appropriately triable elsewhere was long practiced in the courts of New York and some other states. Growth of the practice was retarded by the fear of the federal constitutional provision that "The Citizens of each State shall be entitled to all Privileges and Immunities of citizens in the several States." [117] There were early dicta to the effect that the right to sue was such a privilege. But those doubts would seem today to have little foundation. The Court has expressly said that a state court "may in appropriate cases apply the doctrine of *forum non conveniens*." [118] It has sustained refusal to entertain a cause of action arising out of the state, even under the Federal Employers' Liability Act, where the parties were a nonresident plaintiff and a foreign corporation defendant.[119] It sustained refusal to furnish a forum to enforce a judgment of a sister state obtained by one foreign corporation against another.[120] Suit by a nonresident plaintiff against a railroad in a state where it was neither incorporated nor operating on a contract cause of action not arising in that state has met with such disapproval as in one case to be held an unlawful bur-

---

non Conveniens in Anglo-American Law (1929) 29 COLUMBIA LAW REV. 1; Foster, *Place of Trial—Interstate Application of Intrastate Methods of Adjustment* (1930) 44 HARV. L. REV. 41.

[117] U. S. CONST. Art. IV, § 2.

[118] Broderick v. Rosner, 294 U. S. 629, 643 (1935); Williams v. North Carolina, 317 U. S. 287, 295, n. 5 (1942).

[119] Douglas v. New York, N. H. & H. R. R., 279 U. S. 377 (1929).

[120] Anglo-American Provision Co. v. Davis Provision Co., 191 U. S. 373 (1903). *But cf.* note 39, *supra.*

[55]

den on interstate commerce.[121] The case in my opinion really is a *forum non conveniens* case and only incidentally a commerce clause case. The Court has ordered federal courts, on what seem to me substantially *forum non conveniens* grounds, to relinquish decision of cases within their jurisdiction [122] or to hold them for appropriate decision by state courts to avoid conflict.[123] It would seem that a state court is not obliged to undertake to determine foreign law application to imported causes of action between nonresident parties, at least if a practical remedy is available elsewhere.

Also, in a limited class of cases the Supreme Court has interpreted the due process clause to permit a state to reach absent parties by constructive service, which is almost equivalent to extraterritorial service of process. An interesting example of the growth of constitutional law in this direction is the evolution of the doctrine that entry into a state to do business may have jurisdictional consequences similar to those that flow from domicile. The trend began when it was held that a foreign insurance company, which then had no right to enter the state except with its consent,

[121] Davis v. Farmers Co-operative Equity Ass'n, 262 U. S. 312 (1923). *But cf.* International Milling Co. v. Columbia Trans. Co., 292 U. S. 511, 517 (1934); B. & O. R. Co. v. Kepner, 314 U. S. 44, 51, 58 (1941).
[122] Railroad Commission v. Rowan & Nichols Oil Co., 311 U. S. 570 (1941); Burford v. Sun Oil Co., 319 U. S. 315 (1943); *cf.* Meredith v. Winter Haven, 320 U. S. 228 (1943).
[123] Railroad Commission v. Pullman Co., 312 U. S. 496 (1941); *cf.* Thompson v. Magnolia Petroleum Co., 309 U. S. 478 (1940).

[56]

by entering business was deemed to have assented to a state statute authorizing service on a resident agent in suits based on policies written therein.[124] The following is an interesting sequence: [125] in 1855 the Supreme Court sustained jurisdiction on this implied consent theory; [126] in 1882 it reached the same result on both the consent theory and a doctrine that the corporation by doing business in the state was present there; [127] in 1893 it dropped all mention of consent; [128] and in 1897 it went wholly on the doctrine of corporate presence in a case quite impossible to reconcile with the consent theory.[129] With occasional harking back to the implications of consent,[130] the Court since the turn of the century has reached a new but firm ground of state jurisdiction in no way dependent on expressed or implied consent. It holds unequivocally that carrying on business by a corporation within a state in such a way as to manifest its presence will support the service of state process,

[124] Lafayette Ins. Co. v. French, 18 How. 404 (U. S. 1855); Pennsylvania Fire Ins. Co. v. Gold Issue Mining Co., 243 U. S. 93 (1917). This was based on the theory that the state could exclude the company entirely—a basis somewhat impaired by United States v. South-Eastern Underwriters Ass'n, 322 U. S. 533 (1944), but the result had already come to rest on other grounds.
[125] Pointed out by Cahill, *Jurisdiction over Foreign Corporations* (1917) 30 HARV. L. REV. 676, 692.
[126] Lafayette Ins Co. v. French, 18 How. 404 (U. S. 1855).
[127] St. Clair v. Cox, 106 U. S. 350 (1882).
[128] *In re* Hohorst, 150 U. S. 653 (1893).
[129] Barrow Steamship Co. v. Kane, 170 U. S. 100 (1898).
[130] *E.g.*, Old Wayne Mutual Life Ass'n v. McDonough, 204 U. S. 8 (1907).

[57]

and this although the presence there is solely to engage in interstate commerce.[131]

A natural consequence of this evolution as to corporations was that attempts should be made to obtain jurisdiction of individuals in the same fashion. The Court in 1919 said no,[132] but in 1935 it decided that in some circumstances it would be permissible to gain jurisdiction of an individual engaged in business within a state by service upon his agent.[133]

A comparable development of doctrine has taken place as to the automobile driver in a state where he does not reside. First it was held that the state might forbid him to use its highways without a license.[134] Since it could do that, it was next held that it might forbid him to operate unless he designated an agent for service of process.[135] Then it was held that a state might by statute make mere use of its highways by a nonresident operate as the appointment of a public official as agent for service of process in suits growing out of accidents occurring during such use.[136] Thus, the Constitution has come to be construed to permit a state to obtain jurisdiction in some of those classes of cases which are appropriately tried in the

[131] International Harvester Co. v. Kentucky, 234 U. S. 579 (1914), a doctrine embraced by Judge Cardozo in Tauza v. Susquehanna Coal Co., 220 N. Y. 259, 115 N. E. 915 (1917).
[132] Flexner v. Farson, 248 U. S. 289 (1919).
[133] Doherty & Co. v. Goodman, 294 U. S. 623 (1935). See also Dubin v. City of Philadelphia, 34 Pa. D. & C. 61 (1938).
[134] Hendrick v. Maryland, 235 U. S. 610 (1915).
[135] Kane v. New Jersey, 242 U. S. 160 (1916).
[136] Hess v. Pawloski, 274 U. S. 352 (1927).

[58]

place of the transaction despite the defendant's absence and nonresidence.

But these growths of constitutional doctrine have been based on provisions other than the one we are considering. As to most of that instrument, there has been no reluctance to follow the teaching of Judge Cardozo that "The law, like the traveler, must be ready for the morrow. It must have a principle of growth." [137] But as to extraterritorial recognition or nonrecognition of state law, it is doubtful if a century and a half of constitutional interpretation has advanced us much beyond where we would be if there had never been such a clause. Local policies and balance of local interest still dominate the application of the federal requirement.[138] This is the more strange since the states have less to fear from a strong federalist influence in dealing with this than with most other constitutional provisions. The Federal Government stands to gain little at the expense of the states through any application of it. Anything taken from a state by way of freedom to deny faith and credit to law of others is thereby added to the state by way of a right to exact faith and credit for its own.

It seems easier for the Court to put aside paro-

[137] CARDOZO, THE GROWTH OF THE LAW 20.
[138] Alaska Packers Ass'n v. Industrial Accident Comm'n, 294 U. S. 532 (1935); Pacific Employers Ins. Co. v. Industrial Accident Comm'n, 306 U. S. 493 (1939); Klaxon Co. v. Stentor Electric Mfg. Co., 313 U. S. 487 (1941); Griffin v. McCoach, 313 U. S. 498 (1941); Pink v. A. A. A. Highway Express, Inc., 314 U. S. 201 (1941).

chialism and to think in terms of a national economy or of a national social welfare than to think in terms of a truly national legal system. Perhaps that is because federalism in the field of faith and credit does not have the watchful and powerful championship of the Federal Government, to whose interests the Justices have often been made alert by prior experience in federal office. In contrast, the federalism of the faith and credit clause depends generally on private advocacy, not always supported by the best research and understanding, and often finds the perception of the Justices unsharpened and their perspective uninformed by any extensive experience or investigation of this subject. I confess as much for myself, and my debt to you for your invitation to deliver this lecture—apart from the honor, which I appreciate—arises from the better, but still inadequate instruction acquired in preparation. It is difficult in the pressure of work to orient the contentions in a particular instance with the very broad and indefinite implications of the clause. Even today the literature on it is neither abundant nor well organized. Criticisms of the Court's work in law reviews—which, I agree with Judge Cardozo, is often helpful [139]—seem to me less penetrating and less constructive in this than in other fields. I doubt, too, if it has much emphasis in the law school curriculum.

But the full faith and credit clause is the foundation of any hope we may have for a truly national

[139] See CARDOZO, THE GROWTH OF THE LAW 13–16.

system of justice, based on the preservation but better integration of the local jurisdictions we have. If I have any message to the legal profession worthy of the occasion, it is this: that you must not suffer this lawyer's clause to become the orphan clause of the Constitution.

Bei Fragen zur Produktsicherheit wenden Sie sich bitte an:
If you have any questions regarding product safety,
please contact:

Walter de Gruyter GmbH
Genthiner Straße 13
10785 Berlin
productsafety@degruyterbrill.com